THE WARMTH IN HIS HEART

Deborah J. Merrill

Illustrated by
Amy Barrett Bates

DESERET BOOK

Salt Lake City, Utah

To my children
Deana, Rebecca, Jennifer, Brock, Mindy, and Dustin
and my sweetheart, Terry

First printing in hardbound 1999
First printing in paperbound 2003

DESERET BOOK is a registered trademark of Deseret Book Company

Visit us at DeseretBook.com

ISBN 978-1-57008-540-6 (hardbound)
ISBN 978-1-59038-215-8 (paperbound)

Printed in the United States of America
CDS Publications Inc., Medford, Oregon

10   9   8   7

The party was over. His friends had gone home. Broken balloons, gift paper, and bows cluttered the floor. Cupcake wrappers and half-filled cups of punch were all that remained of the tasty treats. The boy smiled a big oversized smile as he thought of the noise and laughter he had shared with his friends this day. Today was a special day, for today he was eight.

His mom and his dad moved the toys from the couch, then motioned to the boy to come sit with them.

"There is one more gift," his dad said, "but you must choose whether you want this gift or not. Now that you are eight, you may be baptized and become a member of Jesus' church. If you do this you will receive the special gift. It is not wrapped fancy with pretty paper and bows. It isn't something you can see. It is priceless, but money cannot buy it. It won't wear out like other presents do, and you won't out-grow it like the shirt Grandma gave to you. You could lose it like any precious gift, but if you do, you will know where to find it. It is the gift of the Holy Ghost."

A warm feeling came over the boy. It started in his heart and filled his entire body. His mind told him that this would be a great and wonderful gift. And the boy knew he would be grateful for the gift he would be given at the age of eight.

The next Saturday the boy and his family went to the Church. All dressed in white, his dad led him into the waters of baptism.

After drying off and putting on his Sunday-best clothes, the boy and his dad entered the room where his most special people waited. They all smiled at him as he walked up the aisle.

The boy took his seat in the only chair at the front of the room. His dad and several other men with priesthood power put their hands upon his head and he became a member of The Church of Jesus Christ of Latter-day Saints. Then he received the special gift—the gift of the Holy Ghost.

The boy was a good boy. He was honest. He prayed. He did things for others. He always tried to be the best he could be.

After school one day the boy rushed into the house. There was his mom with tears in her eyes. And there at her feet was his dog, laying cold and lifeless in a box. He loved his dog, its yips and yaps. He loved the way it would pounce on the ball after a short chase. He loved the way it felt when the dog was next to him as they both rested in the sun on a summer afternoon. He thought his heart would break.

The boy and his mom found a pillow and put it in the bottom of a wooden box. Then his mom tucked some pretty blue satin over it. They laid his dog on top. The boy thought it was beautiful and an honorable way to bury his dog.

When the boy's dad came home from work that day, they dug a hole and placed the box in it. After covering the box with dirt the boy and his mom and his dad sang a song and said a prayer. They thanked Heavenly Father for the joy the little dog had brought.

A warm feeling came over the boy. It started in his heart, then filled his entire body. His mind told him that his little dog was happy and being watched over. And the boy was grateful for the gift he was given at the age of eight.

The boy grew. He continued to do what was right. He obeyed his mom and his dad. He was respectful of others. He served others whenever he was asked.

When the boy was twelve he was happy to be a Boy Scout. He loved the activities he shared with his friends. His favorites were the campouts and hikes in God's glorious mountains. He loved to listen to the babble of the stream. He laughed as he skipped rocks on the lake. The scent of tall skinny pine trees filled his nose, and silence filled his soul as he watched the doe with her newborn fawn.

One day he laughed as he chased a squirrel over the rocks, up the trees, and around the bushes. He would scurry after, almost catch up, then fall behind again. Breathless, he sat down on a rock to rest. He giggled and panted as he thought of the bushy-tailed squirrel dashing this way and that.

Then he listened. He heard only silence, no voices of the others. He looked around to find them. Surely he could spot the smoke from their campfire. Fear seized him as he realized he was lost. "What do I do now?" he thought to himself. "Help me find the way!" he pleaded to his Heavenly Father.

A warm feeling came over the boy. It started in his heart, then filled his entire body. His mind told him to stay on the rock and wait. He waited. And he waited. The sun became dim, and the evening winds began to stir, when finally he heard a voice call his name. And the boy was grateful for the gift he was given at the age of eight.

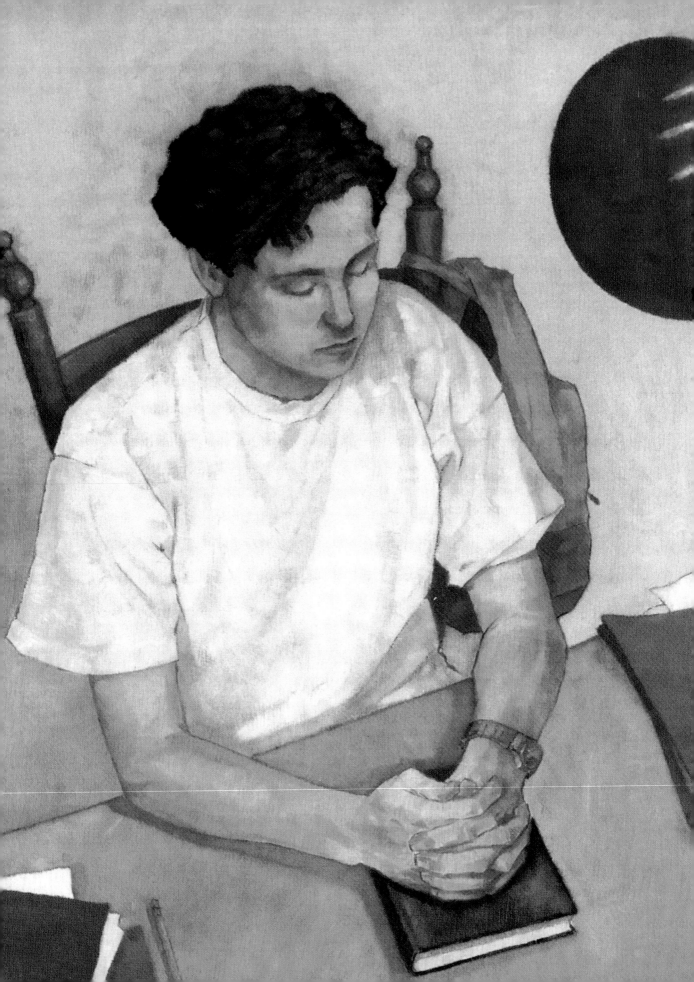

And the boy grew. He studied and he prayed. He did his part for family home evening because his family was important to him. He always wanted to learn more about his Heavenly Father and Jesus.

When the boy was fourteen he enrolled in seminary. He listened to his teacher. He led the singing. He could scripture chase as fast as anyone. He even read his scriptures at home each night.

Then track started. There was homework to do. There never seemed to be enough time to do all he needed to do. He was too tired to read his scriptures.

One day the boy's home teacher gave him a challenge—a challenge to read the Book of Mormon. Then he was to pray to know of its truthfulness. Each month the caring man would check on his progress. The boy liked challenges, so he accepted. He read, not only in the evening but also whenever he had a spare moment. And when he finished, he prayed. He prayed to know whether the book was true.

A warm feeling came over the boy. It started in his heart, then filled his entire body. His mind told him that the book was true. He must find time to read it. It would guide him and be an answer to many of his prayers. And the boy was grateful for the gift he was given at the age of eight.

And the boy grew. He went to church every Sunday. He blessed the sacrament. He paid his tithing. He attended firesides and youth conferences. He chose friends who did the same things.

When the boy was sixteen, he spent more time with his friends than with his family. They went to school together. They played basketball and baseball and hockey together. They went to church dances. They even had their first dates together.

One night the boy's friends decided to go to a party. They wanted the boy to go with them. It was at the house of a boy who was not their friend. He did things that the boy and his friends had been taught not to do. The boy's friends said they would stay for just a little while. But the boy said no, he did not want to go. The boy's friends went to the party, and the boy went home.

A warm feeling came over the boy. It started in his heart, then filled his entire body. His mind told him that he had chosen the right, that it was easier to avoid questionable situations than to deal with the consequences that might result. And the boy was grateful for the gift he was given at the age of eight.

And the boy grew. He finished school with good grades. He continued to read and study and pray. He kept friends who had righteousness in their hearts and supported him in his righteous endeavors. He served others without being asked. The boy also wanted to serve his Heavenly Father.

When the boy was nineteen, he went on a mission. He studied. He fasted and prayed. He followed the mission rules. He taught people about God's eternal plan. Some listened. Some didn't. But he always worked hard.

One day the boy became discouraged. His new companion wasn't there for the right reasons. The weather was rainy, day after day. The letters from his special girl were fewer and further between. It was Christmas day and he wanted to be with his family. Christmas was meant to be spent with the ones you love most. He went to his closet and closed the door. And there he cried his heart out—first, to himself; then, to his Heavenly Father.

A warm feeling came over the boy. It started in his heart, then filled his entire body. His mind told him that God's gift to man was the Christ child that was born on Christmas day. Great would be his joy and numerous his blessings as he shared the message of God's Son with those who had not heard it. And the boy was grateful for the gift he was given at the age of eight.

And the boy grew. Not in stature, but in those things that changed the boy to a man. He desired a home with a wife of his own. He yearned for little ones to raise with love and with care. He asked the Lord to lead him, that his prayers would be answered. And they were.

The man met a young woman who not only was pleasing to look at but also had great beauty within. She was someone he could laugh with, and cry with, and share his deepest feelings with. He knew he was incredibly blessed to find someone as precious as she. His eyes filled with tears as he knelt across the altar from her in the temple of the Lord. There, they pledged their love to each other for all eternity.

The man loved being a husband. He brought home a paycheck. He mowed the lawn and painted the house. He repaired the fence and the car. He took his wife on weekly dates and prayed with her each morning and night. They thought their love was complete when a baby girl joined them in their earthly home.

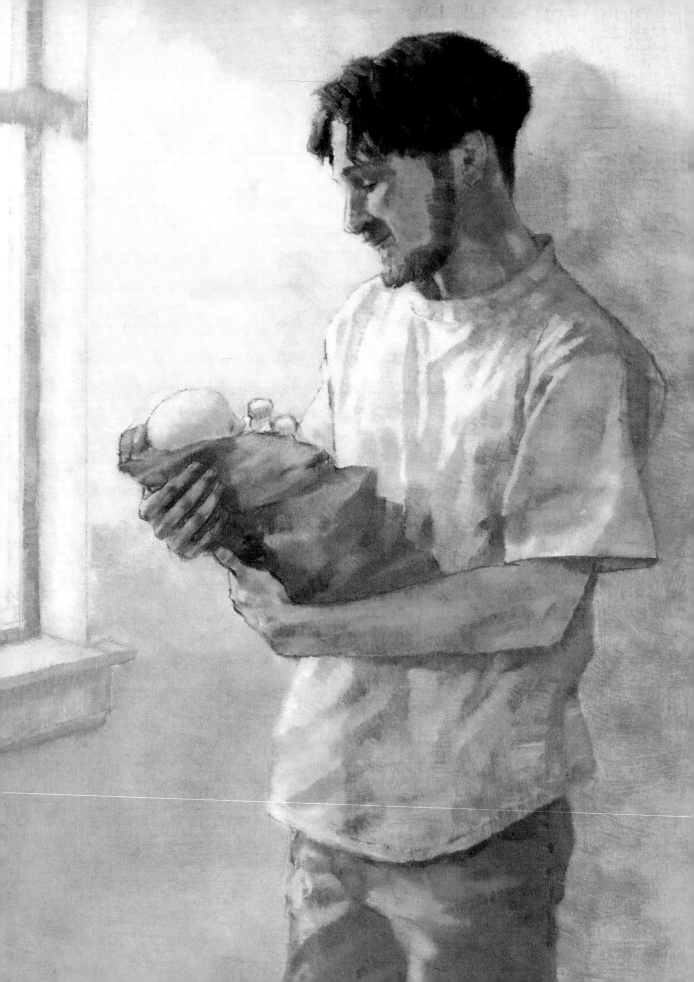

He fed this little girl. He changed her. He helped with her every need. He tickled her, and chased her, and taught her the sounds the animals make. Each night as he rocked her and sang her a song, he thanked God for this wondrous little miracle that had come into their home.

One day the man heard a voice. "Go to the yard now!" The man dashed out the front door. There by the side of the busy road was his baby, not knowing of the dangers that lurked only tiny footsteps away. The man ran to her and gathered her up to the safety of his arms.

And a warm feeling came over the man. It started in his heart, then filled his entire body. His mind told him that his child had been saved because he didn't question or hesitate. Tears flowed. And the man was grateful for the gift he was given at the age of eight.

And the man grew in the experiences that life brought his way. More children came to his home. He taught them righteousness and gratitude. He taught them how to pray to a kind and loving Father. He showed them that he loved their mother and taught them to listen and to obey her. Together, the parents taught their sons and daughters how to work and to play.

One summer day the man and his wife took their children to the lake. They had a wonderful time swimming and splashing in the water. They built sand castles on the shore. They ate their picnic food in the shade of a tree. The day was one they would all remember.

The car was loaded with water toys and wet towels and sandy children. They sang silly camp songs and told jokes as they drove to their home. A large truck filled with scrap metal and garbage pulled beside them to pass. As the truck pulled ever so slightly ahead, the man felt an urgency to slow and let the truck pass quickly. The distance widened, until the man knew it was safe to resume his usual speed. Without warning, a huge sheet of metal flew off the truck and into the road ahead. The man steered his car around it, and they continued on their way.

And a warm feeling came over the man. It started in his heart, then filled his entire body. His mind told him that he was blessed for immediately heeding the prompting. He and his family were protected because he knew the voice inside his mind. And the man was grateful for the gift he was given at the age of eight.

And the man grew in wisdom. He knew what was important. He could counsel his children as they came to him for help. He was pleased at the adults they had become. They knew how to pray and loved the Lord, for the man and his wife had taught them well. And the children brought great joy to the man, and the man was a great blessing to them.

The time came when the children made homes of their own, and there were just the man and his wife together again. They still had weekly dates and candlelight dinners on anniversaries. They still held hands when they walked in the park. They shared each other's trials and each other's successes. They were truly a pair that after so many years had become one, not only with each other but also with God.

And it was time for God to call one of them home. And the man was sad that it was not him. As he knelt at the grave of this angel who had been his beautiful young bride for so many years, he felt an emptiness like none he had felt before. He placed a bouquet of flowers. They were pink and dainty and fine—as was she. And he cried, for he didn't know how to go on.

A warm feeling came over the man. It started in his heart, then filled his entire body. His very being told him that she was his not only for time but also for all eternity. He must continue to do those things that he had always done. He must pray. He must study. He must do good things for others. And when his time came he would be with his lovely wife again. And the man was grateful for the gift he was given at the age of eight.

And the man grew old. He studied and prayed and did good things for others, as he had for so many years.

But the old man was tired—tired and weary. He missed his wife. His children visited often, but that was not enough. The old man began to feel discouraged and wondered why he was still here.

But that was only for a moment. He thought of the marvelous things he had learned: about a loving God and His Son Jesus Christ; about a place where he would live forever with the ones he loved; about eternal progression. He thought of the prayers he had offered and the help he had received. He thought of happy memories with laughing children and a wonderful wife. He thought how much he had been given in the course of a lifetime.

A warm feeling came over the man. It started in his heart, then filled his entire body. His mind told him that he had been good and faithful in doing the things the Lord had commanded. Soon he would join his wife in paradise. From there, they would one day return home to their Father. And the man was grateful for the gift he was given at the age of eight.